Richard Scarry's Please and Thank You Book

A Random House PICTUREBACK®

Richard Scarry's

Please and

Library of Congress Cataloging in Publication Data: Scarry, Richard. Richard Scarry's Please and thank you book. (A Random House Pictureback) SUMMARY: series of stories featuring Huckle, Lowly, Pig Will, Pig Won't, and other characters who demonstrate the good will generated by nice manners. 1. Behavior—Fiction Title. II. Title: Please and thank you book. PZ7.S327Rm 1978 [E] 73-24 ISBN:0-394-83306-6 (B.C.); 0-394-82681-7 (trade); 0-394-92681-1 (lib. bdg.).

H I J

Thank You Book

It's time to read a story!

RANDOM HOUSE NEW YORK

THE BUSY DAY

Huckle and Lowly got out of bed.
They washed their faces and brushed their teeth.
(Lowly didn't have any hair to comb.)

After dressing, they put
away their pajamas very neatly.

At breakfast they chewed
their food slowly and quietly.

When they had finished,
they asked to be excused
from the table. *Everyone*
helped Mommy to clear the table.

Thank you, Lowly

Then all the children went off to school.
Little Sister's shoelace came untied.
Everybody waited while Lowly tied it for her.

At school their teacher
was waiting to greet them.
"Good morning, Miss Honey,"
they all said, cheerfully.

Miss Honey asked them to copy
some words from the blackboard.
When they were done, Lowly
helped Miss Honey by cleaning off
the blackboard.

cat

During recess they all went out
into the schoolyard to play.
They took turns going down the slide.

(That Lowly is certainly a fine slider, isn't he?)

In the afternoon everyone cut up
pieces of colored paper and pasted
them together to make pictures.

B-R-I-I-N-N-G-G! The school bell rang.
Time to go home! Lowly helped Little Sister
clean up her desk. He takes good care of her
because she is younger than the others.
Don't spill the paste, Lowly!

On the way home Lowly
fell into a mud puddle.
Poor Lowly!

He left muddy footprints
all over Mother Cat's clean floor.
"Lowly," said Mother Cat.
"You *know* you should never come
into the house with a muddy foot."

She had to give Lowly a bath.
My! He's a slippery little fellow.

Brrrrr!

Then she dried him off,
and he got dressed for supper.

At the supper table, everyone
ate with his fork. Nobody ever
eats with his fingers or his foot.

After supper Daddy gave everyone
a piggyback ride to bed.
Good night, all!

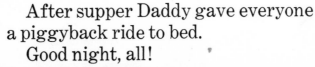

PIG WILL
AND
PIG WON'T

Mother Pig had two little pigs—
Pig Will and Pig Won't.
Whenever she asked them to do something, Pig Will said, "I will."
But Pig Won't always said, "I WON'T!"

If Daddy asked them to play more quietly,
Pig Will said, "I will." But Pig Won't said, "I WON'T!"

When Mother asked, "Will someone please empty
the wastebasket?" who do you suppose said, "I will"?

One day Daddy said, "Who will come to the boatyard and help me work on my boat?"
Pig Will said, "I will."
Guess who said, "I won't."

So Daddy and Pig Will drove
to the boatyard to work.
And Pig Won't stayed home.

Mother Pig stayed in her room
all afternoon writing a children's book.
She paid no attention to Pig Won't.

He had no one to play with.
He had no one to talk to.
Pig Won't spent a very boring
afternoon.

But everyone at the boatyard was working together busily and having a good time.

Pig Will helped Daddy paint his boat.

He helped Bananas Gorilla build a Bananaboat.

He helped Sally Bunny varnish her water skis.

Willy Bear hoisted him
to the top of the mast
on his sailboat. There
Pig Will fixed
the wind vane.

Hard workers get very hungry.
So everyone stopped to have ice cream.
(Oh, dear! Somebody forgot to bring the napkins.)

When Pig Will got back home, he told Pig Won't about the good time he had had. Suddenly Pig Won't began to understand that work—especially if you are helping others—can be lots more fun than doing nothing.

"I must stop saying 'I won't' all the time," he told himself.

Well . . . the very next day his mother asked if someone would help her sweep.
Right away Pig Will said, "I will."
And right away Pig Won't said, "ME TOO!"

I will!

ME TOO!

So from that day on, Pig Won't has always been called "Pig Me Too"!

A VISIT WITH TILLIE

Tillie called some friends and invited them to her house for a little tea party. Bugdozer was already there.

When they arrived at Tillie's house, Huckle shook hands with her and said politely, "How do you do?" The other guests all did the same.

All, that is, except Lowly. He had to shake his foot with Tillie.

Harry Hyena picked up Tillie's big, beautiful vase and waved it around. Tillie had to ask him to put it down. It isn't a good idea to pick up other people's valuable things without asking permission.

Then Tillie asked them all to sit down while she went to get some cake and ice cream.
"Lowly! Stop rocking back and forth in that chair!" said Little Sister. "You are supposed to sit up straight when you are eating at the table."

When Tillie brought in the cake, she asked Lowly to get her a chair.

Lowly brought her a chair.
But it was his own tiny chair
instead of Tillie's BIG chair!

CRASH! Just look what happened.
"Oh, my," said Lowly. "That's
one chair I'll never rock on again."
Tillie laughed. "You won't be
able to *sit* on it again either,"
she said.
Then they all laughed.
They were glad Tillie wasn't angry.

When the party was over,
they all said, "Thank you
for the very nice time, Tillie."
And Lowly even blew her a kiss.

SERGEANT MURPHY'S SAFETY RULES

Here is an old friend—Sergeant Murphy. He has a few good rules everybody should learn . . . and obey.

Always fasten your seat belt in case the car stops suddenly. Little Sister's doll wasn't wearing a seat belt. Poor dolly!

Cross the street at the cross walk when the light tells you that you should.

Never chase a ball into the road.
You might be hit by a car.
Ask an older person
to get the ball for you.

Don't lean out of the window
when you are riding in a car.

Don't run on crowded sidewalks.
Don't push people either—even
for fun. Someone may get hurt.

Don't play near the water.
Sergeant Murphy had to jump
into the water to save Ralphie
Raccoon. Very good, Murphy!

Don't throw sticks or stones at people.
You can hurt somebody that way.

Sergeant Murphy had to put
a bandage on Walter's head.
He bought him an ice cream cone,
too. Wasn't that nice?

Never, never play with matches.
Sergeant Murphy arrived just in time
with that hose!

Sergeant Murphy tells his family to be
careful at home, too. His little girl,
Bridget, knows she should stay away
from the hot stove when Mrs. Murphy
is cooking.

But Bridget doesn't know she should
not leave toys lying on the stairs.
Poor Sergeant Murphy!

"I'm sorry, Daddy.
I won't do it again."

DOLLY'S BIRTHDAY PARTY

Lowly, Huckle, and Little Sister were all invited to Dolly Pig's birthday party.

They brought birthday presents to give to Dolly, and they put on their very best clothes.

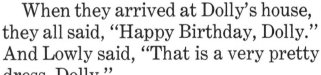

When they arrived at Dolly's house, they all said, "Happy Birthday, Dolly." And Lowly said, "That is a very pretty dress, Dolly."

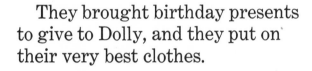

When Dolly began to open her gifts,
her brother cried because he didn't
have any presents. He should be patient.
When his birthday comes, he will have
lots of presents to open, too.
Dolly thanked everybody for the gifts.

Then came the birthday cake.
First, Dolly made a wish.
After that she blew out the candles.
(She almost blew away the cake!)

They could hardly wait to eat
the beautiful birthday cake.
And the ice cream too! Lowly loves
ice cream. Do you?

Later, they played Pin the Tail on the Donkey. Each child took a turn, and the youngest went first. That is the polite way to do things.

Who do you suppose won? . . . LOWLY! He pinned the tail closest to where it was supposed to go. He won a very nice prize, too.

But *somebody* must have thought Lowly was the donkey. Look at his tail! "Ha! Ha! Ha!" laughed Lowly. "What a crazy donkey *I* am!"

At last it was time for the party to end. Lowly remembered to say to Dolly and her mother, "Thank you for a very nice time." He is a very polite little donkey, isn't he?

LOWLY WORM'S
HORRID PESTS

Lowly Worm knows some really Horrid Pests.
He hopes you aren't one of them.

Be careful! You'll break it!

Here is a Selfish Pest.
He won't share his tricycle with his friend.

Who threw that?

PLEASE
PLACE
RUBBISH
HERE

This is a Litterbug Pest.
He throws his rubbish everywhere.

horrors!

And here is a Gobbling Pest.
Don't be like that rude fellow.
Take small bites and chew slowly.
Keep your mouth closed while eating.

I would never eat like <u>that</u>!

You cad!

Look at the Grabby Pest!
He took Little Sister's ice cream, but
Grandma is going to catch him with her umbrella.
Don't take things that don't belong to you.

Never pick on children
smaller than you are.
That is being a mean Bully Pest.

You leave my brother alone!

Don't start to talk
when others are already
talking. You will be an
Interrupting Pest.
   Just say politely,
"May I ask you something?"
Or, "May I tell you something
about that?"

Stop teasing Lowly!
   He's my friend!

A Teasing Pest is just awful!
Nobody likes to be called names.
And sticking out your tongue isn't
very pretty either.

A Noisy Pest is always shouting
and giving people headaches.
No one likes to have a headache.

Lowly also hates Quarreling Pests...

and Fighting Pests...

and Smashing Pests!
They spoil all the fun.

And don't be a Cry Baby Pest
when you lose at games or don't
get what you want.
Lowly Worm *never* cries!

Be a
good
loser!

There are also Driving People Crazy Pests. When their parents tell them they can't do something, these pests just keep pestering and saying, "Why?...Why can't I?" over and over again.

why?

Whining Pests are very annoying, too. Don't whine and carry on if something doesn't work the first time you try it.

Let's go!

Well, that's enough pests. Let's look at some Good Friends and Neighbors for a change.

GOOD FRIENDS and NEIGHBORS

Good Friends and Neighbors always help each other.
Right now all the Bunny Family are trying to help Grandma
find her glasses. Where in the world could she have put them?

Pig Will and Pig Me Too are
also Good Neighbors. When someone
asks them to do something, they
do it right away—with a big smile.

AAAACHOOO!

Good Friends always cover their noses when sneezing or coughing. But it's hard for Eddie Elephant to cover *his* nose when he sneezes. Look out for germs, everyone!

What does Lowly always say when he asks for something?

Please?

May I?

Thank you!

And what does Lowly say when someone gives him something?
Do you say that, too? Good for you!

If you have a friend who is sick, visit him or send him a card. Tell him you hope he gets well soon.

Share with others if you would like others to share with you.

Everyone likes to receive presents.
Give a present to someone once in a while.
Kisses make very nice presents.
But don't be stingy. Give a BIG kiss!

When you are leaving somebody's house after a visit, always remember to say, "Thank you for the very nice time."
Lowly even blows a kiss when *he* leaves.

Go to bed as soon as your parents tell you it is time. No one should have to be told a dozen times.

All right, Lowly!
Please take off your hat and shoe when you go to bed.
Good night, everyone.
Sleep tight!

Just a minute!
I have to get a glass of water!